MXJC

W9-CKC-176

MILITARY SHIPS
CRUISERS

BY JOHN HAMILTON

VISIT US AT
WWW.ABDOPUBLISHING.COM

Published by ABDO Publishing Company, PO Box 398166, Minneapolis, MN 55439.
Copyright ©2013 by Abdo Consulting Group, Inc. International copyrights reserved in all
countries. No part of this book may be reproduced in any form without written permission
from the publisher. A&D Xtreme™ is a trademark and logo of ABDO Publishing Company.

Printed in the United States of America, North Mankato, Minnesota.
032012
092012

Editor: Sue Hamilton
Graphic Design: Sue Hamilton
Cover Design: John Hamilton
Cover Photo: United States Navy
Interior Photos: All photos United States Navy.

ABDO Booklinks
Web sites about Military Ships are featured on our Book Links pages. These links are
routinely monitored and updated to provide the most current information available.
Web site: www.abdopublishing.com

Library of Congress Cataloging-in-Publication Data

Hamilton, John, 1959-
  Cruisers / John Hamilton.
     p. cm. -- (Military ships)
  Includes index.
  Audience: Ages 8-15.
  ISBN 978-1-61783-521-6
  1. Cruisers (Warships)--United States--Juvenile literature. I. Title.
  V820.3.H26 2013
  623.825'30973--dc23
                    2012005061

TABLE OF CONTENTS

CRUISERS

United States Navy cruisers are large warships. They work closely with other kinds of warships to control the seas. Cruisers use advanced weapons and electronics to attack enemy forces.

The USS Port Royal *sails from its home base in Hawaii to a mission in the western Pacific Ocean.*

Cruisers often work in groups, but they are powerful enough to act as flagships of their own attack groups.

TICONDEROGA-CLASS CRUISERS

The Navy has 22 cruisers in its fleet. They are all Ticonderoga-class vessels. The USS *Ticonderoga* was launched in 1981. It is no longer in service. Newer Ticonderoga-class cruisers use the most sophisticated electronics and advanced weapons. Their crews are well trained.

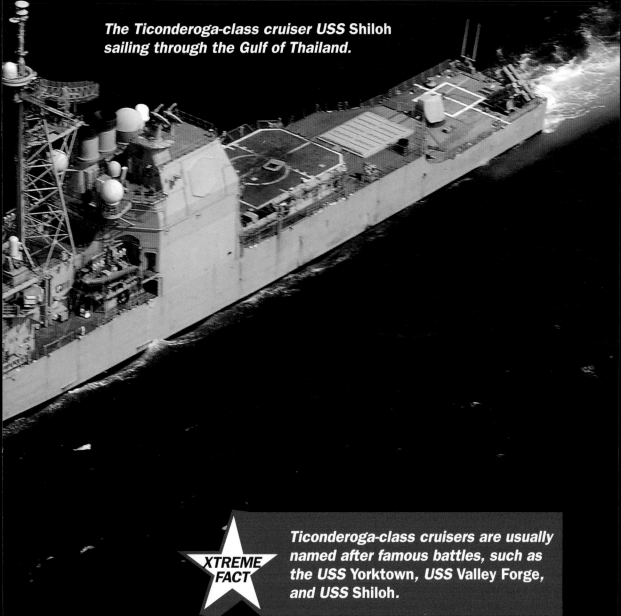

The Ticonderoga-class cruiser USS Shiloh sailing through the Gulf of Thailand.

XTREME FACT

Ticonderoga-class cruisers are usually named after famous battles, such as the USS Yorktown, USS Valley Forge, and USS Shiloh.

MISSIONS

Ticonderoga-class cruisers can perform many missions. Their main job is to protect the fleet from air attacks. Cruisers use advanced radar and missiles to shoot down enemy aircraft.

Ticonderoga-class cruisers are also capable of using missiles to attack other ships, submarines, and land targets.

A test of a Standard Missile Three (SM-3) is conducted from the USS Shiloh.

HISTORY

Before the 1980s, naval warships used large-caliber guns to attack enemy ships and land targets. Aircraft and long-range missiles made these ships obsolete.

A World War II-era battleship fires its guns.

The U.S. Navy needed to protect its fleet of aircraft carriers and other ships. It built guided-missile cruisers, which combine advanced missiles, radar, and computers. These ships appear lightly armed. In reality, they are extremely powerful and versatile.

The USS Ticonderoga, the first guided-missile cruiser of its class, conducting sea trials in 1982.

XTREME FACT

Much of the U.S. Navy's expansion after World War II was in response to threats from the Soviet Union during the Cold War.

CRUISERS FAST FACTS

Ticonderoga-Class Specifications

Length:	**567 feet (173 m)**
Width (beam):	**55 feet (17 m)**
Displacement (loaded):	**10,752 tons (9,754 metric tons)**
Propulsion:	**Four gas turbine engines, two propeller shafts**
Speed:	**30-plus knots (35 mph/56 kph)**
Crew:	**24 — Officers**
	340 — Enlisted

The USS Monterey sailing through the Mediterranean Sea.

ENGINES

Four 80,000-horsepower (59,656 kw) gas turbine engines propel cruisers quickly through the water.

Navy mechanics check a gas turbine engine aboard the USS Anzio.

XTREME FACT

The engines used in Ticonderoga-class warships are similar to the engines used in DC-10 aircraft.

Ticonderoga-class cruisers are heavy. They weigh more than 10,000 tons (9,072 metric tons). But with their powerful engines turning two huge propellers, cruisers can reach speeds greater than 30 knots (35 mph/56 kph).

AEGIS COMBAT SYSTEM

Ticonderoga-class cruisers are often called Aegis cruisers. Aegis is a complex weapons system. It uses advanced radar and computers to track enemies and guide missiles to their targets. The AN/SPY-1 radar is a hull-mounted array that looks for threats all around the ship. It detects enemy air targets more than 288 miles (463 km) away. The Aegis system can track more than 250 targets at the same time.

XTREME FACT

Aegis (pronounced ee-jis) is named after the shield of the Greek god Zeus.

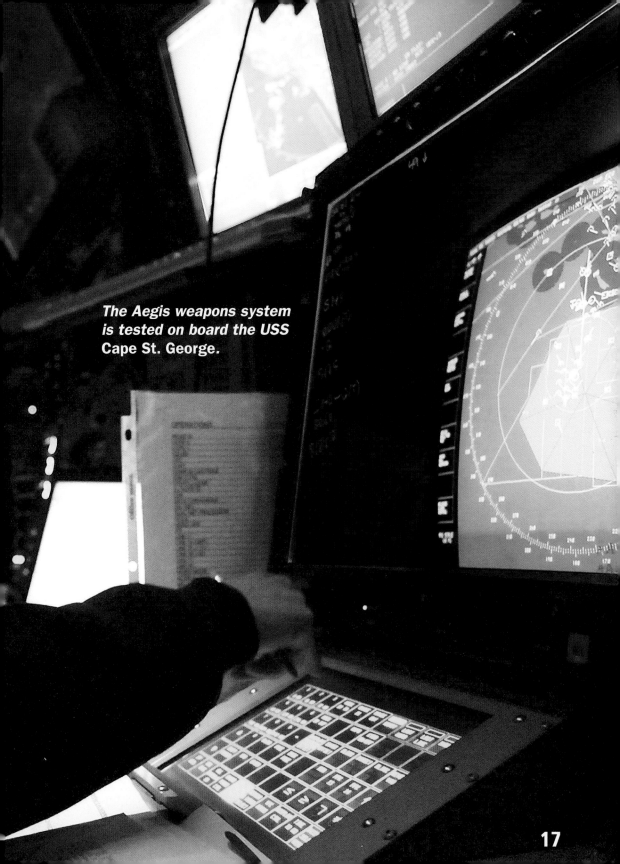

The Aegis weapons system is tested on board the USS Cape St. George.

SM-2 MISSILES

The main mission of a Ticonderoga-class cruiser is anti-air warfare. It protects itself and other Navy ships from enemy missiles and aircraft. The cruiser's first line of defense are SM-2 Standard missiles.

A SM-2 Standard missile launching from the USS Gettysburg.

Missiles are launched from a Mark 41 Vertical Launch System (VLS) underneath the main deck of the cruiser.

SM-2 Standard missiles can intercept enemy targets up to 104 miles (167 km) away. They can be launched even in bad weather. The ship's radar helps guide the missiles to their targets.

PHALANX CIWS

When an enemy aircraft or missile gets too close, Ticonderoga-class cruisers use the Phalanx CIWS close-in weapon system.

It is a rapid-fire gun. It automatically tracks enemy targets. It has a range of about 2.2 miles (3.5 km). Its Vulcan Gatling gun can shoot 75 rounds per second. It uses tungsten armor-piercing rounds that destroy most missiles. Cruisers have a Phalanx CIWS on each side of the ship for maximum protection.

XTREME FACT

Because of its shape and swiveling motion, the Phalanx system is often nicknamed R2-D2 after the Star Wars droid.

HARPOON MISSILES

When attacking enemy ships, Ticonderoga-class cruisers often use RGM-84 Harpoon missiles. They are fired from the stern (back) of the ship. Harpoon anti-ship missiles fly close to the water. That makes them hard for the enemy to shoot down. Harpoon missiles can avoid friendly ships on the way to the enemy.

XTREME FACT

When a Harpoon missile gets close to its target, it activates on-board radar. The radar directs the missile to a precise impact point on the enemy ship.

TOMAHAWK CRUISE MISSILES

When attacking far-away sea targets, cruisers use TASM BGM-109 Tomahawk cruise missiles. They have a range of about 288 miles (463 km). They receive targeting information from satellites.

A Tomahawk missile is launched from the USS Cape St. George.

A BGM-109 Tomahawk missile strikes a warehouse-size test target.

TLAM BGM-109 Tomahawk missiles are similar to TASMs, but they attack enemy land targets. They use radar to compare ground features with an electronic computer map of the target. They can travel about 1,000 miles (1,609 km) to deliver their powerful explosive payloads.

XTREME FACT

Both TASM and TLAM Tomahawk cruise missiles use the cruiser's Mark 41 Vertical Launch System (VLS).

MK 45 GUNS

Ticonderoga-class cruisers are armed with two Mk 45 5-inch (12.7 cm) guns. They are mounted on the front (bow) and back (stern) of each ship's main deck. The Mk 45's main job is to defend against enemy ships. It can also attack aircraft or targets on shore. The Mk 45 can hit targets up to 13 miles (21 km) away.

A live-fire gunnery exercise tests the Mk 45 gun aboard the USS Lake Champlain.

The Mk 45 gun is operated by a crew of six. They load and operate the gun belowdeck.

ANTI-SUBMARINE WARFARE

Stealthy submarines are always a threat to Navy surface ships. Ticonderoga-class cruisers use advanced sonar and torpedoes to defend against these wolves of the sea.

The fast attack submarine **USS** Tucson *traveling the Pacific Ocean with U.S. Navy cruisers and destroyers.*

Landing in rough weather is dangerous. Sea Hawks can drop a steel cable. They are then winched to the small flight deck of the cruiser.

Cruisers can extend the range of their submarine detection by using LAMPS Mk III Sea Hawk helicopters. Sea Hawks can drop sonar buoys. When a sub is detected, Sea Hawks can drop Mk 46 torpedoes to destroy the enemy.

A Sea Hawk helicopter landing on the USS Anzio.

GLOSSARY

COLD WAR

A period of tension and hostility between the United States and its allies versus the Soviet Union, China, and their allies after World War II. The Cold War ended after the Soviet Union collapsed in 1991.

DISPLACEMENT

Displacement is a way of measuring a ship's mass, or size. It equals the weight of the water a ship displaces, or occupies, while floating. Think of a bathtub filled to the rim with water. A toy boat placed in the tub would cause water to spill over the sides. The weight of that water equals the weight of the boat.

ENLISTED

A military service person who joined the armed forces, but is not an officer.

FLAGSHIP

The ship in a fleet, or group of ships, that carries the commanding officer and flies the command flag.

HULL

The hull is the main body of a ship, including the bottom, sides, and deck.

RADAR

A way to detect objects, such as aircraft or ships, using electromagnetic (radio) waves. Radar waves are sent out by large dishes, or antennas, and then strike an object. The radar dish then detects the reflected wave, which can tell operators how big an object is, how fast it is moving, its altitude, and its direction.

SEA TRIAL

The first test cruise of a newly constructed ship. It is the last step in construction. Also called a "shakedown cruise," this first trip at sea may last from a few hours to several days. The ship's speed, maneuverability, equipment, and safety features are tested.

SONAR

Technology that allows ships and submarines to detect objects underwater by measuring sound waves. An "active sonar" system sends out a burst of sound, a "ping" that travels through the water. When the sound wave hits an object, such as a ship or underwater obstacle, the wave is reflected back. By measuring the reflected wave, sonar operators can determine the object's size, distance, and heading. "Passive sonar" detects the natural vibrations of objects in water. It is most often used by submarines, because sending out an active sonar signal might give away the submarine's position.

TOMAHAWK CRUISE MISSILE

A missile that can be launched from a ship, as well as from aircraft or submerged submarines. It has stubby wings, and can be used over medium- to long-range distances.

INDEX